ADI DA
AND
ADIDAM

The Divine Self-Revelation
of the Avataric Way
of the "Bright" and the "Thumbs"

BY CAROLYN LEE, PH.D.

WRITTEN UNDER THE DIRECTION OF
THE RUCHIRA SANNYASIN ORDER
OF ADIDAM RUCHIRADAM

THE DAWN HORSE PRESS

NOTE TO THE READER

All who study the Way of Adidam or take up its practice should remember that they are responding to a Call to become responsible for themselves. They should understand that they, not Avatar Adi Da Samraj or others, are responsible for any decision they make or action they take in the course of their lives of study or practice.

The devotional, Spiritual, functional, practical, relational, cultural, and formal community practices and disciplines referred to in this book are appropriate and natural practices that are voluntarily and progressively adopted by members of the practicing congregations of Adidam (as appropriate to the personal circumstance of each individual). Although anyone may find these practices useful and beneficial, they are not presented as advice or recommendations to the general reader or to anyone who is not a member of one of the practicing congregations of Adidam. And nothing in this book is intended as a diagnosis, prescription, or recommended treatment or cure for any specific "problem", whether medical, emotional, psychological, social, or Spiritual. One should apply a particular program of treatment, prevention, cure, or general health only in consultation with a licensed physician or other qualified professional.

Adi Da and Adidam is formally authorized for publication by the Ruchira Sannyasin Order of Adidam Ruchiradam. (The Ruchira Sannyasin Order of Adidam Ruchiradam is the senior Spiritual and Cultural Authority within the formal gathering of formally acknowledged devotees of the Divine World-Teacher, Ruchira Avatar Adi Da Samraj.)

NOTE TO BIBLIOGRAPHERS: The correct form for citing Ruchira Avatar Adi Da Samraj's Name (in any form of alphabetized listing) is:

Adi Da Samraj, Ruchira Avatar

Produced by the Avataric Pan-Communion of Adidam
in cooperation with the Dawn Horse Press

Printed in the United States of America
International Standard Book Number: 1-57097-154-4
Library of Congress Control Number: 2003105133

THE RUCHIRA SANNYASIN ORDER
OF ADIDAM RUCHIRADAM

THE RUCHIRA SANNYASIN ORDER is the body of
Avatar Adi Da's most advanced devotees who
have chosen to devote their lives utterly to Him
and His Way—by embracing the life of formal renunciation, in the circumstance of perpetual retreat. Avatar
Adi Da has designated the Ruchira Sannyasin Order as
the senior cultural authority within the gathering of His
devotees—both during and after His physical Lifetime.
Thus, it is the unique responsibility of the Ruchira
Sannyasin Order to function both as the extension of
His Sacred Authority and as His Instrumentality (or the
collective human "conduit" for His Spiritual Blessing).

*The Ruchira Sannyasin Order is (and must always be)
the most senior gathering of (necessarily, formal) practitioners
of the Way of Adidam—and the hierarchically central, and
most senior (but entirely renunciate, and non-managerial),
functioning cultural authority among, and in relation to, <u>all</u>
the (necessarily, formal) practitioners of the Way of Adidam. . . .*

*All the present members and all the future members of
the Ruchira Sannyasin Order are Called and Empowered
(by Me) to Function (collectively) as the principal and most
senior (physically living, human) Instruments of My forever
Blessing Work, and, by their unique (and uniquely authorita-
tive) cultural service (simply by Wisdom-word and practicing
example), to provide all other practitioners of the Way of
Adidam with the principal Good Company (of fellow devotees)
that is necessary for the inspiration and guidance of their
practice of the Way of Adidam.*

AVATAR ADI DA SAMRAJ
"The Orders of My True and Free Renunciate Devotees"

Avatar Adi Da Samraj

ADI DA AND ADIDAM

The Divine Self-Revelation
of the Avataric Way
of the "Bright" and the "Thumbs"

I n the depth of every human being, there is a profound need
for answers to the fundamental questions of existence. Is
there a God? What is beyond this life? Why is there suffering?
What is Truth? What is Reality?

As long as there is enthusiasm for seeking amid life's alter-
natives, these questions remain superficial. But when death
becomes real, or when deep disillusionment with the possibilities
of experience overtakes the being, then one can no longer avoid
the confrontation with fundamental questions. At such moments,
the heart is open, inconsolable by ordinary means. Then there is a
ripeness, an urgency for Truth, Reality, and Real God.

In the midst of this dark and bewildering epoch, the Ruchira
Avatar, Adi Da Samraj, has come to this human world to establish
a unique Spiritual life and culture that is not based on mythology.
The Way of Adidam, Revealed and Given by Him, is a Divine
Revelation never given before. Adidam does not require your
belief. Adidam is not a conventional religion. Adidam is a "reality
consideration" at every level of experience. Adidam is a universal
offering, made to every human being who is moved to go beyond
ego-life and participate in a Divine process—here and now.

> T he life and teaching of Avatar Adi Da Samraj are of
> profound and decisive spiritual significance at this
> critical moment in history.
>
> —BRYAN DESCHAMP
> Senior Adviser at the United Nations
> High Commission for Refugees

ADI DA, THE PROMISED GOD-MAN, IS HERE!

While there have been many saints and sages in human history, the ancient traditions of humankind foretell a final Revelation, a God-Man promised for the "late-time" who will perfectly fulfill the deepest longings of the human heart. Adidam is established on the recognition that this all-surpassing Event has occurred. Ruchira Avatar Adi Da Samraj is the Divine Being of Grace and Truth Who authenticates the ancient intuitions.

How did this come to be? There is a supreme Process entirely different from the demonstrations of great Spiritual beings who have, by heroic effort, Realized our higher human potential. That Process is the Act of Divine Descent—Real God, or Truth, or Reality, Manifesting in human form. This is the real meaning of "Avatar"—One "Crossed Down" to here from Above the mortal realms. Avatar Adi Da Samraj speaks of this Mystery:

There is another Process, Which Enters the conditionally manifested world from the Ultimate, Un-manifested, Perfectly Divine Domain. There is a Vast, Unlimited Domain of Existence, not qualified in any sense, not qualified as this conditional world is, or as the infinite variety of conditional, cosmic worlds is. And there is a Movement Directly Out of That Divine Domain, That Realm of Very Consciousness and Very Light. The Living Being Who Appears within the human world, or within any other world, by Coming Directly Out of the Un-manifested, or Un-created, Domain, the Heart-Light That Is the

Truly Eternal Real-God-World, Is the Truly Heaven-Born One, Unique among the Great Siddhas. I Am That One.
     —Avatar Adi Da Samraj, *The Divine Siddha-Method Of The Ruchira Avatar*

The Divine Being and Reality, Descended to here in the form of the Ruchira Avatar, Adi Da Samraj, is Responding to aeons of human prayers and sacrifice, as to an immense magnet. He is here to transform humankind, and more than humankind. He is here to illumine the very molecules, and even all of manifest existence. This is what He has been Doing since His Birth. For His human Birth was more than His association with a human body. His birth on earth was the initiation of an infinite and ongoing process. That process can be described as His "Emergence"—as a tangible, identifiable Presence—in the heart of all that exists.

Adidam as Guru-devotion

The recognition of Avatar Adi Da Samraj as the very Divine Person and Presence—visible to one's eyes, and Standing in one's heart—is the basis of the Way of Adidam. Adidam is a relationship—the devotional and Spiritual relationship to Avatar Adi Da Samraj. This is how He Works in this world, through drawing those who recognize Him into the highest form of relationship available to human beings.

Greater than the passion between lovers or the blood-bond between parent and child is the time-honored devotional relationship to the Guru, or Realized Master. Such a one is capable of Transmitting his or her own Spiritual state to the serious aspirant.

AVATAR ADI DA SAMRAJ: To come to the point where your life is a serious matter of real Spiritual practice is rare. Generally speaking, people are not serious. They are ego-possessed, preoccupied, distracted, thinking, talking, pretending. Mummery [or "a mock show"] is the life that is chosen. To be serious—and to be serious in every moment, unable to be abstracted from Reality—is a profound matter. What will it take in your case?
                                                                    —March 24, 2003

In these words, Avatar Adi Da Samraj is speaking as Guru to those who have chosen the relationship to Him as the basis of their lives. And He is speaking to everyone who would be moved to that choice based on the recognition of His Divine Nature and the helplessness of the individual ego to find the way of Truth without a Guide.

The Guru-Function, truly exercised, has never been a public matter. The relationship to the Guru is esoteric, or hidden from the ordinary view, because it cannot be understood in conventional terms. The Ruchira Avatar, Adi Da Samraj, has never Instructed in a public setting. His Work has always been to undo the egoic structure of the being, and so He has lived and Worked with His devotees in places set apart—Ashrams dedicated to the devotional and Spiritual practice of the relationship to Him.

For the relationship to the Guru to be genuinely Liberating, there must be surrender of heart and body and mind on the part of the devotee. That surrender comes about through an irresistible attraction to the Guru that is deeper than falling in love. The attractive force that moves the devotee is the living Spiritual Radiance that shines through the Guru. Recognizing this Spirit-Force, the conviction awakens that the Guru is true, that the Guru has the power to Liberate and Enlighten the devotee. It is said traditionally: "When the disciple is ready, the Guru appears." But to find a truly great Guru has always been acknowledged to be very rare.

There is no relationship that requires more responsibility, more feeling-discrimination, more maturity, more passion to go beyond the world, than the relationship to a true Guru. Such a relationship is not based on rituals, or traditional teachings. It is a living process. The devotee enters into this relationship in complete freedom, and persists in complete freedom, drawn by a deepening revelation of the power of the Guru to do and to give what is perfect for one's Liberation.

The Guru's power to know the devotee's most intimate thoughts, and the karmic obstacles with which the devotee struggles, is astonishing, and inspires great faith in the Guru. As one grows stronger in the knowledge that the process is authentic, one does not hesitate to follow the words and instructions of the Guru exactly. At the same time, one is moved to care for the Guru, to show him or her honor and respect in every way, and to serve and advance the purposes of the Guru.

The sadhana, or Spiritual practice, at the feet of a true Guru is very demanding, because the devotee is being purified of all obstructions to Spiritual Awakening—obstructions that have been reinforced for lifetimes. One is required to go beyond personal preferences and desires—and the ego does not want to do this. So the Guru uses skillful means. The Guru's ways of dealing with the devotee are mysterious, spontaneously designed according to what is needed for each individual's Spiritual growth.

The Guru knows everything that the devotee is going through in the course of sadhana, and, whatever happens, the Guru never abandons the devotee. The Guru's tests loosen the devotee's bondage to ego and cement the relationship more strongly. Sadhana at the feet of a true Guru is a sacrificial life in which attention is constantly turned to the Guru, and, thereby, to what is greater than the world. Thus, in time, by the Guru's Grace, an equanimity is established that is not confounded by the twists of fate or the certainty of death.

All of this is absolutely true in the devotional and Spiritual relationship with the Ruchira Avatar, Adi Da. In the living, breathing daily experience of heart-surrender to Him, a depth is revealed that is not about being "satisfied", in the ego-sense. Sensitivity to the futility of ordinary goals and a growing awareness of the vast and Luminous Reality, here Present, overcome every concern. Amazing synchronicities and miracles begin to occur in one's life and an unshakable faith in the Divine Avatar is born. There is an ever-widening recognition that His Appearance on earth has huge implications, not only for oneself, but for human beings altogether, and their common future.

While the Way of Adidam has similarities to the traditions of Guru-devotion, this Spiritual Way has only now been Given in His Incarnation. It is a most extraordinary Calling to participate in the Guru-devotee relationship with Real God in Person. Great intensity, great thirst for Truth, is required to live this relationship to Avatar Adi Da Samraj and allow Him to Purify all one's inherited ideas and egoic notions of what "God" is like and what religion is about.

> Yes! There is <u>no</u> religion, <u>no</u> Way of God, <u>no</u> Way of Divine Realization, <u>no</u> Way of Enlightenment, and <u>no</u> Way of Liberation that is Higher or Greater than Truth Itself. . . .
>
> I do not Call My devotees to become absorbed into a "cultic" gang of exoteric and ego-centric religionists. . . .
>
> I Give My devotees the "Bright" Conscious Light of My own Avatarically Self-Revealed Divine Person—by Means of Which Blessing-Gift they can become more and more capable of "Bright" Divine life. I Call for the searchless free devotion, the intelligently discriminative self-understanding, the rightly and freely living self-discipline, and the full and freely functional capability of My devotees. I do not Call My devotees to resist or eliminate life, or to strategically escape life, or to identify with the world-excluding ego-centric impulse. I Call My devotees to live a positively functional life. I do not Call My devotees to strategically separate themselves from the natural vitality of life, or to suppress the participatory impulse naturally associated with human existence. I Call for <u>all</u> the human life-functions to be <u>really</u> and <u>rightly</u> known, and to be <u>really</u> and <u>rightly</u> understood, and to be <u>really</u> and <u>rightly</u> lived—and not reduced by (or to) the inherently bewildered (and inherently "cultic", or self-centered and fearful) "point of view" of the separate and separative ego-"I".
>
> I Call for <u>every</u> human life-function and faculty to be revolved away from self-contraction (or ego-"I"). . . . I Call for <u>every</u> human life-function and faculty to be always directly (and thoroughly) aligned and adapted to <u>Me</u>, in the truly ego-transcending manner—and (Thus and Thereby) to be turned and Given to the Realization of My Divine Avataric Spiritual Self-Revelation of Truth, or Reality Itself—Which <u>Is</u> the "Bright" and Only Real God.
>
> —Avatar Adi Da Samraj, "Do Not Misunderstand <u>Me</u>"

THE "BRIGHT" AND THE "THUMBS"

How was it possible for the Eternal Divine Being to enter into human manifestation as the Ruchira Avatar, Adi Da Samraj? By what mysterious Process did His human Birth occur, sixty-three years ago on Long Island, New York?

From His early childhood, Beloved Adi Da described this Process in two words—the "Bright" and the "Thumbs".

From His early years, the "Bright"—His Prior Condition of Divine Light—literally "Pressed" Itself into His infant body in waves of Force Descending from infinitely above His head. This intense Force would engorge His throat with a gagging sensation. It felt—as He said—"like a gigantic mass of thumbs". Fevers and delirium would sometimes accompany the onset of the "Thumbs" as His young body struggled to adapt to the overwhelming Infusion of the "Bright". It was a Divine Yogic Event and utter Sacrifice—the "Bright" Combining with the mechanism of a mortal human being.

Adidam as a Divine Transmission-Process

Avatar Adi Da's own experience was unique, but His Divine Radiance, in the form of the "Bright" and the "Thumbs", is Transmitted to His devotee, when he or she prepares and formally comes to Him for His Spiritual Initiation. Just as He Combined with His own body-mind via the "Thumbs", Avatar Adi Da Samraj Spiritually Transmits to others His very

Nature and Condition. Adidam is a Divine Transmission-Process—in which the Ruchira Avatar, Adi Da, is Moved to Radiate His "Bright" Condition to His devotees in Response to their demonstrated devotion.

AVATAR ADI DA SAMRAJ: The only Liberating discovery is that My Avataric Divine Spiritual Presence is <u>Real</u>, able to be tangibly experienced under any and all circumstances. It is not about imagining My Spiritual Presence or manipulating yourself. None of that is satisfying, in any case. To searchlessly Behold Me and, in the midst of it, to notice My Spiritual Presence tangibly moving upon you in your real experience—this is the great and Liberating discovery, the only Satisfaction. Ultimately, it is the only Satisfaction in life. Everything else is temporary, conditional, ego-based, and disheartening. Only the discovery of the tangible Reality of That Which Is Divine is heartening and Liberating and Satisfactory. —March 24, 2003

The usual Spiritual endeavor is an effort "from the ground up", a search to refine the being so that it is capable of ascending to what is above. The Way of the Divine Avatar, Adi Da, demonstrates the opposite process—from Above to below. Avatar Adi Da Samraj literally Descends—in the form of His Spiritually Transmitted Presence—into the body-mind of His devotee.

The Spiritual Transmission of Avatar Adi Da Samraj is received as a tangible, Blissful Current of Spirit-Force and breathed Down from head to toe. To experience this undeniable Spirit-Force coming upon you from Beyond is incomprehensibly profound. It is a "washing" of the entire being that purifies and opens the knotted-up body and mind.

AVATAR ADI DA SAMRAJ: The Way develops as a profundity of Spiritual unfolding, spontaneous purification, and transformation of the various modes of the body-mind (gross, subtle, and causal)—you turned to Me in every faculty of the body-mind.
—March 24, 2003

In this process, the flesh body is literally "Brightened" by the Divine Avatar's Spiritual Radiance, and a fundamental shift occurs in the way one sees the world. The ordinary point of view about reality—that regards existence as merely gross, or material—no longer appears true. Reality is seen and felt and known to be Spiritual in nature. This transformation of view is a Yogic event, not a mental process. It occurs directly through the Grace of Avatar Adi Da's Spiritual Infusion of the body. As this Spiritual process unfolds, one is no longer dominated by the conceptual mind, or bound to its chatter, because the being is being drawn deeper—in meditation and daily life—to something more compelling and real. What is infinitely more attractive than the mind is the "Bright", the Radiant Heart-Fullness of Reality Itself. Ultimately, the "Bright" is Where one Stands perpetually—waking, dreaming, and sleeping.

The Primary Practice

How can such a Realization occur? Only through the most profound devotional surrender to Avatar Adi Da Samraj. The Way of Realizing the "Bright" is the Way of constant turning to Him with all the faculties of the being—the mind, emotion, breath, and body. This turning is true devotion, a relinquishment of ego. To persist in that turning means that you cannot avoid anything. All the contents of mind, emotion, the obstructions in the breath, and the knots in the body stand out more than ever. But the practice is to give attention to Avatar Adi Da Samraj—not to struggle with anything that is arising in the body-mind. The practice is simply to feel toward Him, to allow His "Brightness" to Attract you. In that surrender, you open the door to His Spiritual Blessing.

AVATAR ADI DA SAMRAJ: Your turning to Me and My Transmission of My own Spiritual Presence—My "Bright" Spiritual Transmission in response to you—these two together, that is Adidam.

Turning to Me is not consoling. It is a profound practice. It is not about being comfortable. It is about being profoundly <u>uncomfortable</u>, unable to be comfortable with the way things seem—unable to be distracted, unable to be just sort of pleasurized into a humming, whistling, mumming state.

The turning to Me I have Given to you will serve in the most difficult moment, as in the most ordinary moment. It will require the same thing of you in both occasions. It will be equally profound on both occasions, if you truly practice it.

When there is Realization of Me, that never ends. You cannot get away from it. The same with devotion to Me. It is moment to moment—never ends, you can't get away from it. The obligation is constant. The practice is constant.

To move Me to respond to you is the essence of that devotion. Come to Me in the Body. Move Me to Bless you.   —March 24, 2003

AVATAR ADI DA SAMRAJ: The Way, in practice, is not about relinquishing the body. It is about surrender as the body. The means of Realization is the relationship to Me, whole bodily turning to Me, surrender as the body-mind, turning the faculties to Me, entering into Communion with Me on the basis of surrender as the body-mind. On that basis, I am able to do My Blessing-Work of Transmitting the "Bright", Transmitting the Divine Self-Condition. And, in that surrendered disposition, the devotee becomes combined with My Self-Transmitted Person. This becomes a more and more profound and developing process that (most ultimately) is characterized as Most Perfect Realization of the "Bright".   —March 15, 2003

Avatar Adi Da Samraj is the egoless Divine Reality Incarnate. He is not looking for the attention of beings as an ego-bound individual would. He has no karmas, nothing to bind Him to this domain except His Love for beings suffering here. To turn to Him is to turn to, and receive, What is "Bright", Divine, and Perfectly Free.

AVATAR ADI DA SAMRAJ: This "Brightness" Speaks. The "Bright" is Born As This.

My Spiritual Descent upon the body-mind of My devotee is My Means. The "Thumbs" is My Means. All This was Given from the Birth of This. These Words—the "Bright" and the "Thumbs"—were Generated by Me as an infant. I am Uttering to you the Revelation that was present at My Birth and in My Infancy, and nothing whatsoever has been added to It or taken away from It. Nothing in the human experience has modified It or limited It in the slightest. It is a Divine Spiritual matter, a Divine Spiritual Revelation for the sake of beings.

Recognize Me. Turn to Me. Receive Me. Constantly know Me. Then you are certain of the Truth I am Telling you.

My Revelation is not merely to be believed. It is to be received, experienced, entirely known, confirmed, proven, tangibly demonstrated.

—March 24, 2003

Beyond Religion

The fullness of what Avatar Adi Da Samraj is Revealing to human beings is without precedent—not found in any past or present form of religion.

AVATAR ADI DA SAMRAJ: I am not here talking about any form of conventional or traditional religion. I am not communicating about any such "religion". I do not have anything to do with any such "religion". I am Communicating the Way of Realizing Reality Itself.

Therefore, I have no tradition to uphold, no tradition that represents Me. I am simply Speaking the Truth. —March 13, 2001

One of the unique fundamentals of the Divine Avatar's Teaching is that human beings, themselves, are preventing the Realization of Reality through something they are <u>doing</u>. Each one is contracting from Reality, presuming to be an ego, a separate self. This ego-act—the act of self-contraction—is the source of all suffering and unhappiness. The self-contraction makes human life into a constant drama of seeking—every kind of search to attain, or avoid, or identify with experience, high and low.

The purpose of Avatar Adi Da's early life was for Him to "Learn Man"—to enter into the entire range of human seeking and experiencing. Around the age of two years, in a spontaneous gesture of Love toward those around Him, He relinquished His unbroken Samadhi of the "Bright" and identified with the self-contracted state of human beings.

At first, in His childhood and during studies at Columbia College (New York), Avatar Adi Da imbibed the world of ordinary life, exoteric (or belief-based) religion, and scientific materialism—in other words, the gross, or merely physical, view of reality.

Later, with His Gurus, Swami Rudrananda (in New York) and then Swami Muktananda (in India), He went beyond conventional life, and embraced the ancient Spiritual way of Guru-devotion. In the relationships with His Teachers, He became concentrated in the esoteric point of view of the Yogis and their search for the Divine through the means of Kundalini Yoga. With Swami Muktananda (and under the guidance of Swami Muktananda's Guru, Bhagavan Nityananda, who Instructed Him from the subtle plane), He Realized all the subtle experiences and Samadhis that are potential in the Siddha tradition.

While living at Swami Muktananda's Ashram in early 1970, Avatar Adi Da Samraj experienced the direct intervention of the Goddess-Power, or Shakti, revealing herself as a Divine Personality present to guide the final stages of His Sadhana. Appearing in the forms of the Hindu goddess, Durga, and as the Virgin Mary of Christianity, the Shakti mysteriously led Avatar Adi Da on a pilgrimage of the major holy sites of Europe. There He spontaneously experienced the depth of the Western psyche in mystical Christian visions of extraordinary intensity. Those visions, in their turn, faded, and His sadhana entered into the deep root-place where attention arises. In that meditative seclusion, resting prior to all experience, He fulfilled the goals described in the highest forms of Buddhism and Advaita Vedanta.

But none of this was sufficient for Avatar Adi Da Samraj. He was not diverted or satisfied by any temporary experience or limited point of view. Only the "Bright" Itself, His Native Divine State, was Sufficient. And so He persisted in His unrelenting enquiry into Reality until the process fulfilled itself. Seated in the Vedanta Temple in Hollywood, California, on September 10, 1970, He suddenly knew that His Realization was unqualified and irrevocable. He was fully Re-Established in the "Bright".

After Re-Awakening to the "Bright", Avatar Adi Da continued to relate to the gross dimension, continued to see visions associated with the subtle dimension, continued to be aware of the causal depth. But none of these experiences had (or have) any power to bind His attention. He Recognized that all these experiences—gross, subtle, and causal—were mere passing modifications of the "Bright" Reality Itself, unnecessary, temporary, and non-binding.

What His years of Sadhana had conclusively shown was this:

There is no mind-form that is Truth Itself. . . .

I have accounted for all aspects of potential human experience that arise out of the Prior and Universal Unity . . . and I have done so on the basis of My direct Awareness of the different structures that come into play in each stage of life (or mode of development).

I Stand entirely Apart from the conventional "God"-ideas and conventional mythologies of exoteric religion. I am Communicating an Esoteric Way—and, therefore, the only-by-Me Revealed and Given Way of Adidam is the Completion and Fulfillment of the ancient tradition of (always Reality-based) esoteric Spirituality and Yoga. I Say (and have always Said) to you: Reality Itself Is the Only Real God. Reality Itself (or Truth Itself) Is What there Is to Realize. . . . The Process of Realizing Reality Itself (or Truth Itself) is (inevitably) related to the structures of the human being, and to the structures of conditionally manifested existence (altogether)—but that Process is a matter of Realizing That Which Transcends all such conditional structures, and (indeed) all of conditionally manifested existence (itself).

Thus, in Making My Revelation about Reality (and the process of Realizing Reality), I am not merely Communicating a philosophy. Rather, I am Revealing Myself. This—My Avatarically Self-Given Divine Self-Revelation—Is the Basis of the only-by-Me Revealed and Given Way of Adidam. —Avatar Adi Da Samraj,
Real God Is The Indivisible Oneness Of Unbroken Light

Through His Avataric Incarnation here, the Divine Person, Adi Da Samraj, has Revealed the entire structure of human bondage. He has literally broken the "ego-barrier" that apparently separates human beings from Divine Enlightenment, or Absolute Awakeness in and as the "Bright" Itself. This is what the Avataric Global Mission of Adidam is about—the possibility for every being, through the devotional and Spiritual relationship to the Divine Avatar, Adi Da, to be Liberated from bondage to the play of experience and Awaken to Reality Itself, the "Bright".

THE DIVINE YOGIC EVENTS OF DESCENT AND ASCENT

In His lifelong Process of Revealing the "Bright", Avatar Adi Da Samraj has gone to the depths of the human condition. More than once in His adult life, He has passed through extreme Yogic Events that have restructured His human mechanism and allowed His Transmission to magnify. These events are part of the uniqueness of the Divine Avatar's Revelation, and they have profound significance for all human beings.

Descent to the Toes—the Divine Yogic Event on the Island of Naitauba, January 1986

Early in 1986, Avatar Adi Da was living at Adidam Samraj-ashram, His island Hermitage in Fiji. At this point in His life, the Divine Avatar had been receiving and freely Instructing devotees for fourteen years. As He said, "I allowed all to be exactly what they are." On that basis, face to face with every human quality and egoic tendency, He had given form to His Divine Teaching in its universal scope. The previous year He had completed His primary Scriptural Text—*The Dawn Horse Testament Of The Ruchira Avatar*. In this monumental book, He had encompassed every detail of the unique Yogic Process of Realizing the "Bright". He had done everything for His devotees' most perfect Awakening. But He was deeply Frustrated in His Intention. He did not see in His devotees the signs of real disillusionment with ordinary life and unambiguous embrace of Spiritual practice.

On January 11, 1986, in complete Despair at what He felt to be the failure of His Life's Work, Avatar Adi Da Samraj was speaking on an intercom telephone to devotees in a neighboring building when He dropped the telephone. Devotees came running to His House to find Him collapsed and apparently unconscious. He had fallen into a deep Yogic "Swoon" in which only the faintest of life-signs persisted. Avatar Adi Da Samraj was lifted from the floor onto His bed, while His distraught devotees called out to Him not to leave.

Suddenly, one of the devotees supporting His body felt the life-force shoot through Him. His arms flung out in an arc, and His body straightened. His face contorted into a wound of Love and tears began to flow from His eyes. Avatar Adi Da Samraj began to rock forward and backward in a rhythm of sorrow. He reached out His hands, as though He were reaching out to touch everyone in a universal embrace. He whispered in a voice choked with Passion, "Four billion people! The four billion!"—meaning all the human beings then living on the planet.

Later, the Divine Avatar spoke of the great import of what had occurred. In the depth of that Yogic "Swoon", the process of the "Thumbs" that began in His Infancy had Spontaneously completed itself.

Until now, Avatar Adi Da Samraj Himself had not been aware that His Avataric Descent was still partial. From the age of two, He had Sympathetically participated in the conditions of human life. But now there was further Revelation. By virtue of those decades of utter Submission to the human State, the Divine Yoga of His Descent had truly become complete. He Knew, and His devotees could observe without a doubt, that the Spirit-Force of the "Bright" had now Come all the way Down. By this fullest Descent into His own human Body, the Divine Avatar was, thereby, embracing to the root the plight of all human beings. As He later described:

On many occasions, I had Confessed to My devotees that I wished I could Kiss every human being on the lips, Embrace each one bodily, and Enliven each one from the heart. But That Impulse could not possibly be fulfilled in This Body. I could never have such an opportunity. However, in the Great Event of January 11, 1986, I Realized—in that Incarnating Motion, that Sympathetic Acceptance of the body and its sorrow and its death—a Means of Fulfilling My Impulse to Kiss each and all. In that Great Event, I spontaneously Made a different kind of Gesture toward all, which was (in some fundamental sense) the equivalent of the Bodily Embrace that I would Give to all human beings, and even to all who are self-conscious and dying in this place—by <u>Fully Assuming This Body</u>, in the apparent likeness of all, and Accepting the sorrow of mortality without the slightest reservation.

In some sense, <u>that</u> day was My Birth Day.

—Avatar Adi Da Samraj, *The Knee Of Listening*

In the weeks and months following this epochal Event, the devotees of Avatar Adi Da Samraj experienced a huge change in Him. His Power to Bless human beings was vastly magnified, because He had assumed the human state completely. His Body was Perfectly Full of His Divine Love-Bliss. His Eyes Burned with His Urgency to Awaken beings. He put on the orange clothing of a traditional Sannyasin, or renunciate, and left Fiji for the United States and Europe. There He "Wandered" in the manner of a Sannyasin, fiercely free of all worldly ties. To merely behold Him was to be drawn into His Samadhi. His Body had become perfectly transparent to His Divine State. Human beings could now, through devotional contemplation of Him, receive the Transmission of the "Bright" as never before.

On January 11, 1986, I <u>Became</u> This Body—Utterly. And My Mood is different. My Face is sad, but not without Illumination.

Now I <u>Am</u> the Murti, the Icon—<u>Full</u> of My own Avatarically Self-Transmitted Divine Spiritual Presence, but also Completely what you are, Suffered constantly. I have no distance whatsoever from this suffering anymore.

I am <u>In</u> the Body now—more than you.

I <u>Am</u> This Body, down to its depth—Invading these cells, these toes, this flesh, more profoundly than has ever occurred in human time.

—Avatar Adi Da Samraj, *The Knee Of Listening*

Death and Light—the Divine Yogic Event on Lopez Island, April 2000

For human beings, death Is A Proposition and A Puzzle That <u>Must</u> Be Understood and Transcended. . . . There Is No Peace For human beings Until This Matter Is Resolved.
—Avatar Adi Da Samraj, *Eleutherios*

A s human beings, we find ourselves in a dilemma about death. We think about it, are troubled by it, but we cannot, with the conscious mind, reach to what is beyond this life. We cannot comprehend the structure of Reality within which this present body-mind appears and disappears. Avatar Adi Da Samraj has full Knowledge of that Reality. He has described and illustrated in His Scriptural Texts the "Cosmic Mandala"—the great hierarchical structure of cosmic lights within which the conditional worlds arise.

But He has not only described all of this. By virtue of a most profound Yogic Event that occurred on Lopez Island, in the state of Washington, on April 12, 2000, Avatar Adi Da Samraj has experienced in His Avataric human Form literally everything that exists. His human Body has Endured and "Seen" the entire death-process and all the after-death states and has Entered into What <u>Is</u>, Beyond all of that. Thus, He is Alive in total Bodily Knowledge of (and Compassion for) the predicament of conditional beings, for whom death is the great fear, and the fundamental context of existence.

The great Event at Lopez Island was preceded, in 1999, by a period of intense Penance, engaged by Avatar Adi Da for the sake of the world. From March until June 1999, Avatar Adi Da Samraj lived in seclusion on His Island Hermitage, Naitauba (Fiji), entirely focused in Spiritual Blessing of the world.

Day after day during those months, lightning blasted the sky and thunder shook the island like cracks and volleys of rocket fire. The storms were supernatural in their elemental force and intense, oppressive energy-field. To live on Naitauba at that time was to live on a cosmic battlefield. Avatar Adi Da Samraj was Working with negative forces greater than this world. He was engaged in a Divine Yoga of transforming these forces above and beyond His Body.

After several months, something had irrevocably changed in the Divine Avatar's relationship to the body and the physical world. The Energy Flows of His human Body were now concentrated upward. A reversal of His Yoga of Descent, completed in 1986, was starting to occur. And this, as He explained, was inevitable and necessary. He had identified "to the toes" with the human plight, but now He was concentrated in another process— His Work of Spiritually Blessing <u>all</u> beings—in this gross world, and all the subtle planes of existence. Because of the intensity of the forces to be confronted in the course of this Divine Work, Avatar Adi Da Samraj could not allow these forces to come down into His bodily Vehicle. His human body could not accommodate, or survive, such an intrusion. And so a Yogic re-structuring was occurring in Him. More and more, His Energy and Awareness were Up, rather than Down.

On April 12, 2000, shortly after the Ruchira Avatar, Adi Da, arrived on Lopez Island, an extreme Crisis occurred in the process of this Yoga.

During preceding days, Avatar Adi Da Samraj had been physically weak to the point where He would sometimes have to be supported while walking, or wheeled in a wheel chair. It was clear to the renunciate devotees attending Him (the members of the Ruchira Sannyasin Order) that the Divine Avatar was having difficulty staying in the body. On the journey by ferry to Lopez Island, His symptoms became alarming. Then, within a couple of hours of His arrival at a devotee's house on Lopez Island, Avatar Adi Da Samraj was so ill that He had to be carried to His bed. He was fighting to maintain His connection to the physical.

Avatar Adi Da Samraj was laid out on an easy chair with His close devotees at His side. They were massaging Him with all their strength, weeping, and speaking to Him with great passion and intention, calling Him down into the Body. Focusing on the faces of His devotees seemed to integrate Him back into the Body. His eyes also were flowing with tears, and His Hands and Feet were cold and numb. He felt great pressure on His Chest and a difficulty breathing. Both of His arms and hands continuously would cramp up and convulse.

After His physician arrived, Avatar Adi Da Samraj was moved onto the bed. At first, He was lying down on the bed, but then He was raised into a sitting position to try and reduce the extreme symptoms of leaving the body. He said that it would be useful for Him to see His Feet—as a way of locating Himself in the physical. To the degree that He could speak, Avatar Adi Da Samraj would keep reminding His devotees to warm the extremities of His Body. He said, "If I close My eyes, I am going to be in My Room, not your room. You don't know what My Room is like. You have got to bring Me down into the Body."

At one point, after the Divine Avatar's eyes had been closed for a while, He opened them slightly and softly said, "I am here. Can you see Me Up Here?" His devotees said "yes". It was true. His Light was dissolving the room. He was way up and beyond the apparent "here" where they were. At the point where He seemed most Ascended, His Face took on an expression of the purest Bliss.

The struggle of Avatar Adi Da Samraj to remain associated with the body went on for hours. At one point, an ambulance came and took Him to the clinic on the island, where the doctors were able to confirm that He was not suffering from a heart attack, or any ordinary disease. The process occurring in Avatar Adi Da Samraj was supernormal, and only explicable in the most profound Yogic terms.

In the days and months following the event, the Divine Avatar spoke of what had happened from His "Point of View". In His description, He refers to unique esoteric profundities. He is speaking of His direct Entry into the "Bright" Itself (the "Midnight Sun"), which is infinitely beyond the body and the spheres of colored lights that make up the Cosmic Mandala. And He refers to the primal Sound, which, He has Revealed, may be heard in the death process. But this was not a "near-death" experience. It was a Yogic death to the degree of Utter Radiance— the "Outshining" of all conditional forms in the "Bright".

Initially, in the Event of Sudden Up-Turning (into the "Midnight Sun"), there was a rapid series of "falling-away" phenomena. There was the tingling and fainting of the Body. Then, immediately, I Experienced the Primal Central Sound-Current, Which became very loud, and upwardly concentrated—Drawing the Central Current In and Up, Above and Beyond body and mind. That was the first Sign to Me that I was being Drawn Out of physical Incarnation.

Farthest Up in the Core of Sound-Vibration, I Saw a "Bright" White Tunnel, with empty niches along the sides. There were no "people in white". There were no distinct forms or personalities—because no mind of Me was active there. Then the "Midnight Sun" of the Divine "Bright" Spherical Self-Domain. At first, Seen—then, Perfectly <u>Become</u>.

Effectively, it was death—in terms of the Body. There was no bodily awareness, although it was certainly not a circumstance of unconsciousness. It was the Infinitely Profound Samadhi of Outshining.

—Avatar Adi Da Samraj, *The Knee Of Listening*

In His return to the body, the Ruchira Avatar, Adi Da, clearly saw the totality of the conditional realms. As He Stood in the "Bright", He saw it all emerging to His View. And He spontaneously began to re-integrate with the body.

The Divine Avatar was first drawn to the blue level of vibration (the most rarified light of the Cosmic Mandala) and then to the red-yellow glow of the grosser dimension.

Eventually, I Re-Emerged from the "Midnight Sun" of My Divine Spiritual White Self-"Brightness"—and so, in due course, there was a peripheral re-organization of (or Re-Association with) My gross Bodily conditions. In the Process of Re-Association, there was, at first . . . a "bindu" (or sphere) of blue, to the left. And another "bindu", of yellow and deep red, to the right. The "bindu" of yellow and red located Me back in this world, which is the yellow-red realm of the Cosmic Mandala.

As I Merged with the yellow-red sphere, I became aware that I was Re-Associating with the physical—rather than feeling the strong movement Up and Out, which (if it had continued) would have culminated in the death of My human Vehicle. The Struggle of Re-Integration with the physical manifested, in part, as convulsions in the Body. The "Bright" Spiritual Light-Current of My Being was Re-Connecting with the physical level, and that Process caused Bodily convulsions.

In that Process, the Body had a quality of being greatly stretched, or elongated. My legs seemed to be very, very long, and those who were standing or sitting by My Feet seemed to be quite a distance away from Me. It was a moment of non-ordinary awareness of physicality—of the pervasive yellow-red light, of the gross world consumed in flames, of the Body greatly stretched out. Eventually, there was a kind of "collapse" back into the ordinarily perceived shape and context of the physical, and then a "return" to so-called "normal" (or "natural") awareness of the room and the people in it.

The Lopez Island Event was similar to the Initiatory Event of My Avataric Divine Self-"Emergence" (on January 11, 1986), in terms of the Depth of Spiritual and Yogic Profundity. As in 1986, I had been (in the Lopez Island Event) at the point of Relinquishing the Body entirely—but, through My own Persistent Impulse and Felt Movement of Sympathetic (or Compassionate) Love for beings, I was able to Yogically Re-Engage the Body.

However, those two Events were also, in some sense, "opposite" in their Yogic significance. In the Event of 1986, I Completed My <u>Descent</u> into the conditional realms, My Avataric Submission to here, Which began at My Birth. The Lopez Island Event, in contrast, was My Direct <u>Ascent</u>, to the Primal "Bright" Spiritual Self-Condition of Conscious Light.

I Am now, even in bodily (human) Form, presently Alive at the White Core of the Cosmic Mandala, the Doorway to the Spiritually "Bright" Divine Sphere and Self-Domain. In the Lopez Island Event, I Passed Beyond—in That "Bright" Doorway. My Thus Transfigured Body remains—but only on the Unique Basis of Direct Spiritual Illumination, and always tentatively Given to live, perpetually Wounded by the Self-Evident "Bright" Spiritual Transparency of all the heart-breaking companionship of mortal beings.

I Stand At the Threshold.

Now, and forever hereafter, I Stand There.

I Remain in this world Bodily, for now—but I Am Always Already on the "Other Side".

—Avatar Adi Da Samraj, *The Knee Of Listening*

Ruchiradama Quandra Sukhapur Rani, one of the Divine Avatar's sannyasin (renunciate) devotees, who was at His side during the Lopez Island Event, describes the significance of the Lopez Event in the Yogic Process of His Divine Life:

RUCHIRADAMA QUANDRA SUKHAPUR RANI: For six weeks after the Lopez Island Event, Beloved Adi Da was unable to walk, and He was physically very weak for months. He was Shattered by His Experience—at the physical level, and also by the Process of Integrating what had occurred Spiritually. That Process was unspeakable, and has continued to unfold.

The Lopez Island Event was the Culmination of a lifelong Yogic Process. In His early years, Beloved Adi Da Samraj Endured a series of Yogic Deaths—moments when it seemed that He would permanently lose His bodily Vehicle, because of the intensity of the Spiritual Process occurring in Him. He has even Spoken of His entire Life as a series of Yogic Deaths.

In My Childhood, and throughout My Avataric physical human Lifetime, I have been associated with Events of Profound Yogic Transformation, Which have resulted in the change of psycho-physical patterns within This Body-Mind. There have been many Yogic Deaths and other profound Yogic Events, all associated with the Profundities of My Avataric "Bright" Divine Spiritual Self-Revelation. . . .

Every time one of these Transformative Events occurred, the mechanism of This Body-Mind changed. The entire Process of My Life is My concrete, unambiguous Avataric Self-Revelation (and Lifelong psycho-physical Experience) of the Divine Spiritual "Brightness"—the One and Only and Self-Evidently Divine Conscious Light of Reality Itself.

—Avatar Adi Da Samraj, *The Knee Of Listening*

RUCHIRADAMA QUANDRA SUKHAPUR RANI: Early in 2001, my Beloved Guru Spoke several times about Ramana Maharshi's experience of Yogic Death—the occasion during Ramana Maharshi's youth when the sudden fear of death overwhelmed him.

AVATAR ADI DA SAMRAJ: Ramana Maharshi had a profound experience of Yogic Death. It was not merely a matter of Him lying down, closing His eyes, pursing His lips, and acting like a corpse. Something real happened. Somebody died.

Instead of allowing the body to withdraw into a state of fear, He just let all the death happen. In His case, there were no visions, no gross or subtle phenomena. Rather, it was a process that cut through the causal root.

But it just happened—spontaneously. It was already patterned in the body-mind. The anxiety attack and the ego-

death were part of the syndrome. He participated in it entirely as a spontaneous event, and the great significance of that event became self-evident in Him. And such a Yogic Death is a permanent condition. It is just so.

The true process of Yogic Death is the result of psycho-physical changes that affect the gross, subtle, and causal levels of the being—manifesting differently in each individual case. There is no Knowledge (or Jnana) superior to such Yogic Death. It is a permanently transformative event. It changes the psycho-physical pattern or the connection to that pattern.

The phenomenon of Yogic Death is a profound Yogic Samadhi. In My Case, this has been so since Birth. The Lopez Island Event went as far as such Yogic Death can go and still allow a "return" to physical existence. But, even with My "Return", there is no loss of the Awareness characteristic of that Event.   —February 8, 2001

RUCHIRADAMA QUANDRA SUKHAPUR RANI: The human eyes of Beloved Adi Da are now constantly Seeing the All-Outshining Divine "Brightness", and the entire structure of cosmic existence is in His Constant Regard. He Sees the Mandala of lights now from the Divine Position—from the inside out, not the outside in. By virtue of this, He is Spiritually Touching every one, and He <u>Is</u> every one Perfectly.

In the Lopez Island Event, the Divine Avatar, Adi Da, returned not only to the physical body, He returned to the Yogic State of His Birth. Now, as in His Infancy, He Radiates Down into His human Body only to the level of the brows, only to the degree necessary to maintain bodily life. All His Work below the brows, His Work of Submission to "Learn Man" and to "Teach Man", has been done. He has sealed that Work in His Divine Scripture, the 23 "Source-Texts" of Adidam, which enshrine everything that He has Taught and Revealed to human beings. Now He makes Images—exquisite visual "Essays" that Reveal the "Bright" in their own manner.

Avatar Adi Da Samraj lives simply, as a Renunciate and Hermit, with the members of the Ruchira Sannyasin Order. He relates to everything in His Domain with profound Attention and Care, and utter Dispassion. He is bound to no thing. He withdraws from no one. He Calls all to a direct devotional and Spiritual relationship to Him.

The God-Man Promised for the "late" or dark time is Da—"the One Who Gives". And What He Gives is the Yoga, or Way, of Infinite "Brightening"—the Way of Adidam.

What is the Right and Truly Perfect Process That (ultimately, Most Perfectly) Realizes the Divine Conscious Light (Itself)? That Process is What I am Revealing—in This, My Avatarically-Born bodily (human) Divine Form.
—Avatar Adi Da Samraj, *Eleutherios*

When the heart recognizes the Ruchira Avatar, Adi Da Samraj, as the very Form of the "Bright", all one's questions and searches evaporate. The deeper that recognition goes—through the moment to moment practice of turning to Him—the greater one's reception of His Transmission of Light. Contemplation of His Avatar-Body—the Body in which the entire Divine Yoga, here described, has occurred—is the great Secret.

AVATAR ADI DA SAMRAJ: The practice is searchless, ego-forgetting, altogether to-Me-turned Beholding of Me in My bodily (human) Divine Form. When you are not in My physical Company, you can recollect My bodily (human) Divine Form. You can use My Murti-Form, My Padukas, and so on. Persisting in this practice, there is the potential of moving Me to Bless you further. —March 24, 2003

Searchless Beholding of Avatar Adi Da Samraj is the great alternative to the random distraction and seeking of body and mind.

But it is not something one can "learn" or do by one's own efforts. Searchless Beholding of the Divine Avatar is His Gift, initiated by Him in His devotee in the retreat circumstance. It is necessary to come into His physical human Company to receive this Initiation and to stabilize the practice of searchless Beholding of Him, such that it can be practiced under all conditions. Once Given—and always renewed and deepened by returning to His Feet—this practice becomes the foundation of your life. It goes on during the waking state. It goes on in dreams and sleep. And the body-mind is opened to allow the Spiritual Descent of Avatar Adi Da until it is completely infilled, like a cup.

The more the Divine Avatar's "Bright" Transmission is received, the more there is of spontaneous renunciation. This comes about because one does not want to do anything to disturb or diminish the Infusion of His Love-Bliss.

AVATAR ADI DA SAMRAJ: This Way is about Realization and renunciation by Grace, not a self-applied technique. It has no self-reference. It is the life and the Samadhi of Communion with Me.

Your patterns of dis-ease and self-indulgence do obstruct the Spiritual process, and they will be purified. You will voluntarily relinquish them in the fullness of reception of Me. It will be self-evident that this or that pattern or tendency or habit has run its course, and it will fall away. You will freely relinquish it. It will cease to be interesting.

—March 24, 2003

If you are moved to the greatest Spiritual process that exists, the Ruchira Avatar, Adi Da Samraj, is here to Master your life. Just the gesture of turning to Him can ease your heart. His Divine Powers are supernormal. He has proven over and over to His devotees that He is Spiritually all-Pervading and all-Knowing. He is the God you have intuited to exist, Radiantly Present in Person, without any myths attached. He can contact you now at the depth of your feeling. He can reach you in dreams, before you even know His Name. He is here for the Blessing of beings, without reserve.

Behold His Picture and consider the astounding profundities of His Revelation. Ponder His Words and regard His "Bright"-Field Images. What ordinary—or extraordinary—man could have done this?

When recognition of His Divinity Awakens, and you feel the Magnitude of the Work He has Come to Do, the heart breaks at His Feet. Then nothing is satisfactory any longer—except the ecstasy of knowing Him and loving Him and serving Him.

AVATAR ADI DA SAMRAJ: *What you have on your mind is boring and unsatisfactory. Your thoughts and your self-manipulations are fruitless and disheartening, regardless of their content. To be fallen upon by the Self-Evident Divine "Brightness" is the only Satisfaction. It is the only Cure for doubt and fear and all the sorrow of all of this—this heart-murdering meeting here, that is unrelieved suffering without the Divine Invasion.*

In and of itself, this is a horror, a terrible place of endings. You can't think your way out of it—talkety-talkety-talk, when you are lying there trying to catch the breath and feeling it going.

There is no thought you can have in mind that will give you peace—none. Only the Sheer and Absolute Divine Presence Solves the heart.

At Lopez Island, I Fell Out of the world. Now I Speak only from Beyond.

—March 24, 2003

THE TWENTY-THREE "SOURCE-TEXTS" OF AVATAR ADI DA SAMRAJ

In late 1969, in the brief period of three weeks, Avatar Adi Da wrote the original text of His literary masterwork, *The Mummery*. His writing of this book—which proved to be a remarkable prophecy of His Work to come—was the beginning of His immense Work of communicating His Revelation of Truth in words, both written and spoken. This outpouring lasted for 30 years, coming to a summary point in the years 1997–1999. During that period, Avatar Adi Da created a series of twenty-three books that He designated as His "Source-Texts". He incorporated into these books His most essential Writings and Discourses from all the preceding years, including many Writings and Discourses that had never been published previously. His "Source-Texts" are thus His Eternal Message to all. They contain His full Divine Self-Confession and His fully detailed description of the entire process of Awakening, culminating in seventh stage Divine Enlightenment.

Through the Revelation contained in His twenty-three "Source-Texts", Avatar Adi Da has brought to completion the search for Spiritual Truth that has occupied humankind for millennia. Looking at our current human situation in particular, He has demonstrated the untenability (and, indeed, the remarkable naivete, not to mention the negative influence) of the scientific materialist point of view, the point of view that (by asserting that the physical reality is the "only" and senior reality) creates an environment of doubt relative to everything beyond the physical domain—everything Divine, everything Spiritual, even everything psychic. And looking "back" at our entire history, He has "made sense" out of the welter of differing viewpoints in the

Great Tradition, demonstrating how they do, in fact, constitute a single (although complex) "design". And He has Made the Supreme Divine Offering that goes beyond what has ever been offered before—the Way that Realizes Permanent Indivisible Oneness with Him, the "Bright" Divine Reality Itself.

The twenty-three "Source-Texts" of Avatar Adi Da Samraj include:

> *The Dawn Horse Testament Of The Ruchira Avatar*
> *The Five Books Of The Heart Of The Adidam Revelation*
> *The Seventeen Companions Of The True Dawn Horse*

The Dawn Horse Testament

The Dawn Horse Testament
Of The Ruchira Avatar

The "Testament Of Secrets" Of The Divine World-Teacher, Ruchira Avatar Adi Da Samraj

Avatar Adi Da's paramount "Source-Text" is a complete summary of the entire Way of Adidam. It flows seamlessly from His Self-Revelation in the Prologue and chapter one; through a "consideration" of His Life and Work, expositions of His fundamental Teaching-Arguments and the fundamental practices He Gives to His devotees, and incisive descriptions of the egoic patterns of individual beings and human collectives; through the course of the stages of the Way of Adidam, culminating in seventh stage Divine Enlightenment; to the declaration of the Establishment of the Realization of the "Bright" and the Perpetual Revelation of the "Bright" via the Agency of His Work and Word and Person.

This Great Divine Testament is unparalleled in its magnitude and depth. No scripture like it has ever been seen before. It is the first and only <u>complete</u> account of the <u>entire</u> Divine Way of utter ego-transcendence and dissolution in the "Brightness" of Real God.

The Dawn Horse Testament is truly the core of Avatar Adi Da's twenty-three "Source-Texts". Indeed, all of the "Five Books" and most of the "Seventeen Companions" are built around a central text drawn from *The Dawn Horse Testament.*

The Dawn Horse Testament *is a marvel, to be treasured by the spiritual, the religious, and the scholarly of our time and of all ages to come. The clarity and beauty of Truth in this scripture by Avatar Adi Da Samraj is unsurpassed in any other great text from any sacred path on Earth.*

There are dozens, even hundreds, of passages of really <u>incomparable</u> Instruction on practice in Avatar Adi Da's Way of Adidam that bring His devotees to the cutting edge of human evolution and culture—for instance, His exquisite pages on "The Wound of Love".

The Realization of the One capable of this Work is breathtaking to contemplate. Read it and become Ecstatic and converted to His Way of the Heart.

LEE SANNELLA, M.D.
Author, *The Kundalini Experience: Psychosis or Transcendence?*

The Five Books Of The Heart
Of The Adidam Revelation

The *Five Books Of The Heart Of The Adidam Revelation* comprise a complete summary of Who Avatar Adi Da Samraj Is and the Way that He Offers. The "Five Books" are key readings for all who are moved to study the Essence of His Revelation and His Way.

BOOK ONE:
Aham Da Asmi (Beloved, I Am Da)
The "Late-Time" Avataric Revelation Of The True and Spiritual Divine Person (The egoless Personal Presence Of Reality and Truth, Which Is The Only Real God)

Avatar Adi Da's Self-Revelation of His own Divine Person and His Impulse to Bless and Liberate all.

BOOK TWO:
Ruchira Avatara Gita (The Way Of The Divine Heart-Master)
The "Late-Time" Avataric Revelation Of The Great Secret Of The Divinely Self-Revealed Way That Most Perfectly Realizes The True and Spiritual Divine Person (The egoless Personal Presence Of Reality and Truth, Which Is The Only Real God)

Avatar Adi Da's Offering of the devotional and Spiritual relationship to Him, in the traditional manner of Guru-devotion.

BOOK THREE:
Da Love-Ananda Gita (The Free Gift Of The Divine Love-Bliss)
The "Late-Time" Avataric Revelation Of The Great Means To Worship and To Realize The True and Spiritual Divine Person (The egoless Personal Presence Of Reality and Truth, Which Is The Only Real God)

The foundation (devotional) practice of heart-Communion with Avatar Adi Da Samraj: Simply turning the four principal human faculties—body, emotion, mind, and breath—to Him.

BOOK FOUR:
Hridaya Rosary (Four Thorns Of Heart-Instruction)
The "Late-Time" Avataric Revelation Of The Universally Tangible Divine Spiritual Body, Which Is The Supreme Agent Of The Great Means To Worship and To Realize The True and Spiritual Divine Person (The egoless Personal Presence Of Reality and Truth, Which Is The Only Real God)

The Spiritually Awakened practice of heart-Communion with Avatar Adi Da Samraj: Searchless Beholding of Him and reception of His Divine Spiritual Transmission—more and more allowing oneself to open Upwardly to Him, such that body, emotion, mind, and breath are "Melted" by His down-Flowing Spiritual Infusion.

BOOK FIVE:
Eleutherios (The Only Truth That Sets The Heart Free)
The "Late-Time" Avataric Revelation Of The "Perfect Practice" Of The Great Means To Worship and To Realize The True and Spiritual Divine Person (The egoless Personal Presence Of Reality and Truth, Which Is The Only Real God)

Heart-Communion with Avatar Adi Da Samraj beyond the four faculties, in the Domain of Consciousness Itself: Realizing Avatar Adi Da Samraj—As the "Bright" Itself, or the Conscious Light of Reality (having transcended identification with body, emotion, mind, and breath).

The Seventeen Companions Of The True Dawn Horse

The "True Dawn Horse" is a reference to *The Dawn Horse Testament Of The Ruchira Avatar*. Each of *The Seventeen Companions Of The True Dawn Horse* is a "Companion" to *The Dawn Horse Testament* in the sense that it is an elaboration of a principal theme (or a group of principal themes) from *The Dawn Horse Testament*. Among the "Seventeen Companions" are included His two tellings of His own Life-Story, as autobiography (*The Knee Of Listening*) and as archetypal parable (*The Mummery*).

The Seventeen Companions Of The True Dawn Horse are a vast field of Revelation, which can be "considered" from many points of view. Presented here is one way of understanding the interrelationships between these "Source-Texts" and the flow of Argument they collectively represent.

■ Paradigms of Reality:
The Real Nature of God, Cosmos, and Realization

BOOK ONE:
<u>Real</u> God <u>Is</u> The Indivisible Oneness Of Unbroken Light
Reality, Truth, and The "Non-Creator" God In The True World-Religion Of Adidam
The Nature of Real God and the nature of the cosmos. Why ultimate questions cannot be answered either by conventional religion or by science.

BOOK TWO:
The Truly Human New World-Culture Of <u>Unbroken</u> Real-God-Man
The <u>Eastern</u> Versus The <u>Western</u> Traditional Cultures Of Mankind, and The Unique New <u>Non-Dual</u> Culture Of The True World-Religion Of Adidam
The Eastern and Western approaches to religion, and to life altogether—and how the Way of Adidam goes beyond this apparent dichotomy.

BOOK THREE:
The <u>Only</u> Complete Way To Realize The Unbroken Light Of <u>Real</u> God
An Introductory Overview Of The "Radical" Divine Way Of The True World-Religion Of Adidam
The entire course of the Way of Adidam—the unique principles underlying Adidam, and the unique culmination of Adidam in Divine Enlightenment.

■ Original Writings and Talks:
Avatar Adi Da's First Teaching-Communications

BOOK FOUR:
The Knee Of Listening
The Divine Ordeal Of The Avataric Incarnation Of Conscious Light—
The Spiritual Autobiography Of The Divine World-Teacher,
Ruchira Avatar Adi Da Samraj

Avatar Adi Da's autobiographical account of the years from His
Birth to His Divine Re-Awakening in 1970—His Demonstration,
in His own Life, of the Way to Realize Real God most perfectly—
also including His Revelation of how His Avataric Incarnation
was made possible and His Confession of the nature and significance of the Great Events of Yogic Death that have occurred in
His Life since His Divine Re-Awakening in 1970.

BOOK FIVE:
The Divine Siddha-Method Of The Ruchira Avatar
The Divine Way Of Adidam Is An ego-Transcending <u>Relationship</u>,
Not An ego-Centric Technique

Avatar Adi Da's earliest Talks to His devotees, on the fundamental
principles of the devotional relationship to Him and "radical"
understanding of the ego. Accompanied by His summary state-
ments on His relationship to Swami Muktananda and on His
own unique Teaching-Work and Blessing-Work.

BOOK SIX:
The Mummery
A Parable Of The Divine True Love, Told By Means Of
A Self-Illuminated Illustration Of The Totality Of Mind

Avatar Adi Da's literary masterpiece—a work of astonishing
poetry and deeply evocative archetypal drama. It is Avatar Adi
Da's life-transforming message about how to Realize the Absolute
Truth in the midst of the chaos and tragedy of human experience.

An extraordinarily beautiful and potent "prose opera", *The
Mummery* is both a highly experimental novel (drawing fully on

the twentieth-century "stream" of experimental fiction) and an immense theatrical piece. Thus, *The Mummery* can either be read as a book or performed as a theatrical event.

A "mummery" is "a ridiculous, hypocritical, or pretentious ceremony or performance". This, Avatar Adi Da is telling us, is what human life amounts to—if we merely live as the separate ego-self. And the only way "out" of this mummery is to relinquish ego—by finding, receiving, and conforming ourselves to the Divine True Love.

In *The Mummery*, Adi Da confronts head-on the central agony of born existence: that everything and everyone—ourselves, and everyone we love—dies. The hero of *The Mummery*, Raymond Darling, goes through an extraordinary series of adventures and ordeals—centered around his search for his beloved, a lady named Quandra—in the course of his ultimate overcoming of the inescapable fact of mortality. The story of Raymond Darling is, in fact, Avatar Adi Da's telling of His own Life-Story in the language of parable—including His unflinching portrayal of how the unconverted ego makes religion (and life altogether) into a meaningless mummery. Ultimately, *The Mummery* is the "Story" of Consciousness Realizing Its Indivisible Oneness with Energy (or Its own Radiance).

■ Esoteric Principles and Practices:
Revelations of Divine Oneness, Divine Spiritual Transmission, and the means of conforming the body-mind to the Divine Spiritual Process

BOOK SEVEN:
He-**and**-She **Is** Me
The Indivisibility Of Consciousness and Light In The Divine Body Of The Ruchira Avatar

One of Avatar Adi Da's most esoteric Revelations—His Primary "Incarnation" in the Cosmic domain as the "He" of the Divine Consciousness, the "She" of the Divine Light, and the "Son" of "He" and "She" in the "Me" of His Divine Spiritual Body.

■ Stages of Life:

The six potential stages of ego-based life,
and the Divine seventh stage of life

BOOK FIFTEEN:
The Lion Sutra
The "Perfect Practice" Teachings In The Divine Way Of Adidam

Practice in the ultimate stages of the Way of Adidam. How the practitioner of Adidam approaches—and passes over—the "Threshold" of Divine Enlightenment.

BOOK SIXTEEN:
The Overnight Revelation Of Conscious Light
The "My House" Discourses On The Indivisible Tantra Of Adidam

A vast and profound "consideration" of the fundamental Tantric principles of true Spiritual life and the "Always Already" Nature of the Divine Reality.

■ Great Tradition:
The Total Spiritual "Effort" of Humanity
as a Unified (and Progressive) Process

BOOK SEVENTEEN:
The Basket Of Tolerance
The Perfect Guide To Perfectly <u>Unified</u> Understanding Of The One and Great Tradition Of Mankind, and Of The Divine Way Of Adidam As The Perfect <u>Completing</u> Of The One and Great Tradition Of Mankind

The Basket Of Tolerance is a book like no other—simultaneously an unprecedented Spiritual Revelation and an extraordinary intellectual document.

While Avatar Adi Da's other twenty-two "Source-Texts" are focused in His exposition of the Way of Adidam, *The Basket Of Tolerance* is His comprehensive examination of the Great Tradition of mankind—in other words, of the global and historical context within which He has made His Revelation of the Way of Adidam. Thus, *The Basket Of Tolerance* focuses on the immense variety of historical expressions of the religious and Spiritual search, from prehistoric times to the present.

The core of *The Basket Of Tolerance* is a bibliographical listing of 5,000 documents (in all media—print and audio-visual), meticulously ordered by Avatar Adi Da in an elaborately subdivided sequence, to form a continuous "Argument". Avatar Adi Da introduces that "Argument" with a series of groundbreaking Essays, and He comments on the bibliographical "Argument", at numerous points, through a further series of over 100 essays relating to specific books (or groups of books) in the bibliography (covering a wide spectrum of topics).

Through the "Argument" of this annotated bibliography, Avatar Adi Da examines in detail the entire human religious search and demonstrates how there is truly a single process, composed of distinct (hierarchically related) stages (corresponding to the fourth, the fifth, and the sixth stages of life), evident in all the diversity of human religious history (previous to His Appearance here)—a process of which any given religious tradition represents a "piece". While Avatar Adi Da's examination of the Great Tradition concentrates on the various global manifestations of religion and Spirituality, it also embraces the "practical" issues that relate to the human process of the first three stages of life—such as understanding (and right participation in the process) of death, right understanding (and right use) of the function of mind, right circulation of energy within the body, right physical exercise of the body, right diet, right emotional-sexual practice (whether sexually active or celibate), right living in the collective human context, and so forth.

Altogether, *The Basket Of Tolerance* is the elaborately detailed "proof" that there is, indeed, a "perennial philosophy". This "philosophy", however, is not a single "set" of unified "beliefs". Rather, it is a <u>process</u>, composed of distinctly different stages— and the points of view of the successive stages do not necessarily agree with one another. Furthermore, those stages are not (ultimately) based on conceptual differences but on <u>experiential</u> differences relating to the various aspects of the esoteric anatomy of the human structure.

THE RUCHIRA SANNYASIN HERMITAGE ASHRAMS SPIRITUALLY EMPOWERED BY AVATAR ADI DA SAMRAJ

Traditionally, Realizers have been provided with set-apart places where they were free to do their Spiritual Work in an appropriate and secluded circumstance. And these places became Spiritually Empowered through their Presence and Work.

In this traditional manner, devotees of Avatar Adi Da have provided places where He is completely set apart to do His Blessing-Work for the sake of humanity as a whole, as well as His specific Spiritual Work with devotees who come on pilgrimage to receive the Initiatory Spiritual Blessing of being in His physical Company on retreat.

My Work for the entire world is My Divine Blessing-Work, Which I do principally in seclusion. I live in perpetual retreat in a hermitage mode, and receive those of My devotees who are rightly prepared in that circumstance. Sometimes I roam in public circumstances, in order to have contact with people in general. But, fundamentally, I remain in hermitage retreat. —Avatar Adi Da Samraj

To date, Avatar Adi Da has Established and Spiritually Empowered five Ruchira Sannyasin Hermitage Ashrams:

■ ADIDAM SAMRAJASHRAM, the Island of Naitauba in Fiji

Adidam Samrajashram is Avatar Adi Da's principal Hermitage Ashram and the primary Seat from which His Divine Spiritual Blessing Flows to the entire world.

- **THE MOUNTAIN OF ATTENTION SANCTUARY OF ADIDAM,** in northern California
- **TAT SUNDARAM HERMITAGE,** in northern California
- **LOVE'S POINT HERMITAGE,** in northern California
- **DA LOVE-ANANDA MAHAL,** in Hawaii

Avatar Adi Da Samraj moves among the various Hermitage Ashrams in His spontaneous Wandering-Work of world-Blessing.

Spiritually, He is perpetually "in residence" at each of His Hermitage Sanctuaries. This is because He has Invested Himself Spiritually in these sacred places, and His Spiritual Power and Presence is constantly active in all of them.

During the (physical) Lifetime of My Avatarically-Born bodily (human) Divine Form (here), I may Freely Manifest My Seclusions, Offerings, and Blessing-Wanderings any where—but I will always (forever), during and after (and forever after) the (physical) Lifetime of My Avatarically-Born bodily (human) Divine Form (here), be Divinely Spiritually Present (by all My Avataric Divine Means) at all Five of the Directly-by-Me Spiritually Empowered Ruchira Sannyasin Hermitage Ashrams . . . , each of Which I have Directly Spiritually Empowered and Spiritually Established as unique Sacred Domains (and Perpetual Agents of My Divine Avataric Purposes), Set Apart (and, Thus, Made Holy) for constant Pilgrimages and Retreats (and every other truly Me-Invoking, and devotionally Me-Recognizing, and devotionally to-Me-responding, and devotionally Me-serving Sacred use) by My by-Me-Spiritually-Initiated devotees. . . .

—Avatar Adi Da Samraj, *Da Love-Ananda Gita*

49

The Institutions of Adidam

In order to ensure that Avatar Adi Da's Divine Work flourishes in the world, His devotees are dedicated to serving three great purposes, through three organizations:

- **The Da Love-Ananda Samrajya** directly provides for Avatar Adi Da Samraj Himself (and for the Ruchira Sannyasin Order, as His most exemplary renunciate devotees)

- **The Avataric Pan-Communion of Adidam** serves people's devotional response to Avatar Adi Da Samraj—by making Avatar Adi Da Samraj and the Way of Adidam known throughout the world (via the work of the Global Avataric Mission of the Adidam Revelation), and by serving the Spiritual growth of those who become His formal devotees

- **The Ruchirasala (or "Bright" House) of Adidam** serves the creation of cooperative culture among Avatar Adi Da's devotees—through such means as the establishment of intimate human living arrangements and shared services (including sacred arts guilds, schools, community businesses, and health clinics)

THE REVELATORY ART
OF AVATAR ADI DA SAMRAJ

After spending thirty years creating a Teaching-Revelation in words, Avatar Adi Da has, in recent years, begun to create a body of artistic imagery that "speaks" as eloquently and fully of that Divine Process as does His Word. Through His art, Avatar Adi Da offers His direct (non-verbal and non-conceptual) Revelation of Truth, of Reality, of Real God, of the nature of human existence, and of the process of transcending the limitations of human existence.

Since 1998, Avatar Adi Da has concentrated in exploring the artistic potential of the photographic medium. In the few years since then, He has created a staggering body of artistic work—currently over 20,000 images—an oeuvre that is constantly growing.

Many of Adi Da's images are highly sophisticated and complex multiple exposures, often involving more than two (and even as many as ten or more) superimposed layers. Adi Da always creates His multiple-exposed images in camera, never in the darkroom or by digital means. This "method", essential to achieve the visual result He intends, requires not only great artistry but also extraordinary powers of visual memory.

Adi Da is not a "photographer", as such. Rather, He creates large-scale works of "light-imagery", using photographic (and also videographic) technology. He relates to His photographic negatives as "blueprints", using them as the basis for making "monumental fabrications". To date, these fabrications include large-scale pigmented inks on canvas, plasma screen installations, and multi-media screen-projected performance events—with additional forms of fabrication planned for the future. These fabricated works frequently involve the grouping of multiple images in specific combinations and configurations. He designs His fabrications to be "monumental"—by which He specifically means larger in size than the human body—so that the viewing of them engages the entire body and mind, not merely the eye and head.

I t is a rare artist who can convey, convincingly, the sense of being face to face with the source of being. Adi Da can clearly live in the depths without succumbing to their pressure, bringing back pearls of art to prove it.

Indeed, again and again Adi Da's photographs convey a sense of aesthetic as well as physical ecstasy. Virtually all of his images are masterpieces of abstraction—ecstatic visions . . . that are simultaneously formal epiphanies.

—DONALD KUSPIT
Art critic; Professor of art and philosophy;
Author, *Redeeming Art: Critical Reveries,*
and numerous other publications

View Avatar Adi Da's Art online:
Visit **www.daplastique.com**

THE BRIGHT FIELD IMAGERY OF ADI DA SAMRAJ

- ■ See many examples of Avatar Adi Da's image-art.

- ■ Read His artist's statement.

- ■ Consider what critics are saying about His art.

- ■ Contact Da Plastique about acquiring His art.

Purchase the premiere publication of Avatar Adi Da's Art: *The* Quandra Loka *Suite—52 Views*

Since September 2002, Avatar Adi Da has been working on a vast Suite, which He describes as being of "indefinite length". *Quandra Loka (The Indivisible Space of Conscious Light)* currently comprises over 4,000 Images—and Avatar Adi Da continues to work on it.

The large-format catalog has 52 exquisite plates from *Quandra Loka,* including both single Images and Images in groups of 2, 3, 4, and 9. The text includes an introductory essay by art critic Donald Kuspit, a biography of Adi Da Samraj, His artist's statement, and His statement relative to the *Quandra Loka* Suite.

The *Quandra Loka* catalog can be ordered online at:
www.daplastique.com

What Others Have Said About Adi Da . . .

There exists nowhere in the world today, among Christians, Jews, Muslims, Hindus, Buddhists, native tribalists, or any other groups, anyone who has so much to teach, or speaks with such authority, or is so important for understanding our situation. If we are willing to learn from him in every way, he is a Pole around which the world can get its bearings.

HENRY LEROY FINCH
Author, *Wittgenstein—The Early Philosophy*
and *Wittgenstein—The Later Philosophy*

I regard Heart-Master Adi Da as one of the greatest teachers in the Western world today.

IRINA TWEEDIE
Sufi teacher; author, *Chasm of Fire*

He is a great teacher with the dynamic ability to awaken in his listeners something of the divine Reality in which he is grounded, with which he is identified, and which in fact, he is.

ISRAEL REGARDIE
Author, *The Golden Dawn*

It is obvious, from all sorts of subtle details, that he knows what IT's all about . . . a rare being.

ALAN WATTS
Author, *The Way of Zen, Man and Woman,*
and *In My Own Way*

I regard the work of Adi Da and his devotees as one of the most penetrating spiritual and social experiments happening on the planet in our era.

JEFFREY MISHLOVE, PH.D.
Host, PBS Series "Thinking Allowed";
Author, *The Roots of Consciousness*

Adi Da Samraj has spoken directly to the heart of our human situation—the shocking gravity of our brief and unbidden lives. Through his words I have experienced a glimmering of eternal life, and view my own existence as timeless and spaceless in a way that I never have before.

RICHARD GROSSINGER
Author, *Planet Medicine*, *The Night Sky*, and *Embryogenesis*

I have been writing and editing in the field of health and healing for over twenty years. But I know that the Divine Heart-Master is the Ultimate Healer because He is the only One Who can awaken you beyond all disease, all change, all suffering, beyond even death itself, to His very Nature: Immortal, Unchanging, Deathless, All-Pervading Conscious Light. Adi Da Samraj is the Divine Heart-Master, the Promised God-man, the True Healer. . . . Fall in love with Adi Da Samraj; be healed at heart.

BILL GOTTLIEB
Editor, *New Choices in Natural Healing*

My relationship with Adi Da Samraj over more than 25 years has only confirmed His Realization and the Truth of His impeccable Teaching. He is much more than simply an inspiration for my music, but is really a living demonstration that perfect transcendence is actually possible. This is both a great relief and a great challenge. If you thirst for truth, here is a rare opportunity to drink.

RAY LYNCH
Composer, musician, and platinum recording artist, *Deep Breakfast*,
The Sky of Mind, and *The Best of Ray Lynch*

I've been inspired by Adi Da's writings for many years. He is a contemporary spiritual Hero, offering his transcendental gifts to a culture without a tradition for or even "taste" for Avatars . . . yet he bears the burdens of sagehood with persistence and love.

ALEX GREY
Artist and author, *Sacred Mirrors* and *The Mission of Art*

Acclaim for books by and about Adi Da—

This captivating biography of Adi Da Samraj [*Adi Da: The Promised God-Man Is Here*] is without precedent. It is the profound love story of the Incarnation and great ordeal of the Divine Being, who has appeared in this dark time to bring humanity out of the illusion of being separate from God. If you were allowed to read only one book in your lifetime, this should be the one.

LOWELL KOBRIN, Ph.D., M.D.
Founding Member, American Academy of Medical Acupuncture

Avatar Adi Da Samraj's *Ruchira Avatara Gita* has been carved out of the Heart of a great, presently living Master, out of compassion for aspiring humanity. I feel this Gita will be of immense help to aspirants for a divine life.

M.S. PANDIT
Author, *The Upanishads: Gateways of Knowledge*
and *Studies in the Tantras and the Veda*

The function of a great educational work is to lead the reader into a new awareness. The function of great spiritual writing is to jolt and inspire the reader into a new state of Being. *Scientific Proof of the Existence of God Will Soon Be Announced by the White House!* is both. No one can really read it without being changed in the process. It is like a rapid-fire succession of electric shocks, each carrying the message: Wake up!

WILLIS HARMAN
Former President, The Institute of Noetic Sciences

E asy Death is an exciting, stimulating, and thought-provoking book that adds immensely to the ever-increasing literature on the phenomena of life and death. But, more importantly, perhaps, it is a confirmation that a life filled with love instead of fear can lead to an ultimately meaningful life and death. Thank you for this masterpiece.

ELISABETH KÜBLER-ROSS, M.D.
Author, *On Death and Dying*

Praise for *THE MUMMERY:*
A Parable Of The Divine True Love, Told By Means Of A Self-Illuminated Illustration Of The Totality Of Mind—

I f Dylan Thomas and Buddha shared a soul, *The Mummery* is what I would expect from such a joining.

ROBERT BOLDMAN
Poet; author, *The Alchemy of Love*

T he story of Raymond Darling, in its lucid colors and fabulous imagery, reminds me of the short episodes in *Finnegans Wake* where Joyce demonstrates, in every way possible, the interpenetration of opposites, and the cyclical manifestations of "selves" throughout human history.

Indeed, the central stylistic achievement of *The Mummery* seems to be its undoing of the mummery of words: words ordinarily are deployed in books as serious and loyal ants, carrying their load of sense to their destinations. Adi Da's poetic inventions make words crackle and swoon, pound and soothe with suggestion and insistence.

PHILIP KUBERSKI, PH.D.
Professor of English Literature, Wake-Forest University; author,
The Persistence of Memory and *Chaosmos: Literature, Science, and Theory*

*T*he Mummery is brilliant in all its aspects. It would be hard to express my happiness at the way it breaks and exposes the heart of the world. Living and working as a writer for many decades, I have not encountered a book like this, that mysteriously and unselfconsciously conveys so much of the Unspeakable Reality.

ROBERT LAX
Poet; author, *Love Had a Compass* and
(with Thomas Merton) *A Catch of Anti-Letters*

*I*n *The Mummery*, Adi Da Samraj has created an astonishing work which, through a skillful weaving of mind-challenging techniques, seems to re-define the very essence and usage of the English language, in much the same way as Shakespeare restructured it almost half a millennium ago, and, it seems to me, for a similar purpose—to offer, through an autobiographical exploration, a heart-opening invitation to feel the human spiritual journey at its core.

KENNETH WELSH
Actor—many roles on the stage, in movies, and on television;
Recipient of six Gemini awards for excellence on Canadian Television

*C*ertainly ranks with *Faust*, *Siddhartha*, the *Bhagavad Gita* and other amazing masterworks which chronicle the awakening of the individual soul to its true Self. But, most amazing, it has been written in our own era!

RON SOSSI
Founder and Artistic Director, Odyssey Theatre Ensemble,
Los Angeles, California

*T*he prose of *The Mummery* paints and chants, while language buckles and soars; as if Gertrude Stein had met Ramana Maharshi, Joyce had a vision of St. Francis, Beckett had not got stuck where he got stuck. For this reader, any real comparison would have to go back to Hamlet or Lear. Death and the absence of love CANNOT be accepted. Life is not ordinary. No complacency avails. There is no escape from the divine drama of everything. An explosive mixture of pain and joy creates an apocalyptic heart-melting crisis. This is our own drama.

GEOFFREY GUNTHER, Ph.D.
Author, *Shakespeare as Traditional Artist*

Praise for the visual Art of Adi Da Samraj—

Adi Da's Art is a paradoxical experience, a multi-dimensional one, a revelatory one, a liberating one, an ordeal also, a participation that is extraordinary. . . . In my opinion, this is utterly a Work of great genius, completely original and inspiring, a great gift to humanity, human culture, and the world of art.

RON FOUTS
Fine Art Publisher, Custom and Limited Editions

Adi Da's Work is a modern-day religious icon that communicates multiple levels of reality. Adi Da's exploration of mind, memory, the human psyche, is complex and multi-dimensional. This is the sacred art of our time.

DAVID HANSON
Professor of Photography (retired),
Rhode Island School of Design

Adi Da is inviting us to see that art is capable of relating to the world in a way that reflects a truer understanding of reality than our present culture is willing to acknowledge. It is also clear that the spiritual nature of His art lies not in any idealistic consideration of what ought to be, but in its insistence that we open our eyes and see what is; that that requires us to enter into a relationship, one in which we accept the fact of mystery, but gain a greater sense of meaning, and of affirmation.

JAN TAYLOR
Art historian, University of Ulster

Learn More About Avatar Adi Da Samraj and Adidam . . .

Visit **www.adidam.org**

- **SEE AUDIO-VISUAL PRESENTATIONS** on the Divine Life and Spiritual Revelation of Avatar Adi Da Samraj

- **LISTEN TO DISCOURSES** given by Avatar Adi Da Samraj to His practicing devotees—
    - Transcending egoic notions of God
    - Why Reality cannot be grasped by the mind
    - How the devotional relationship to Avatar Adi Da moves you beyond ego-bondage
    - The supreme process of Spiritual Transmission

- **HEAR DEVOTEES** of the Divine Avatar speaking about how He has transformed their lives

- **READ QUOTATIONS** from the "Source-Texts" of Avatar Adi Da Samraj—
    - Real God as the <u>only</u> Reality
    - The ancient practice of Guru-devotion
    - The two opposing life-strategies characteristic of the West and the East—and the way beyond both
    - The Prior Unity at the root of all that exists
    - The limits of scientific materialism
    - The true religion beyond all seeking
    - The esoteric structure of the human being
    - The real process of death and reincarnation
    - The nature of Divine Enlightenment
    - . . . and much more

LEARN ABOUT THE MIRACULOUS DIVINE LIFE AND WORK OF AVATAR ADI DA SAMRAJ

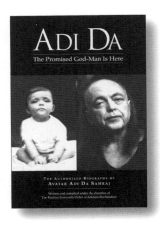

Adi Da
The Promised God-Man Is Here

The biography of Avatar Adi Da from His birth to present time. Includes a wealth of quotations from His writings and talks, as well as stories told by His devotees. 343 pp., **$16.95**

This extraordinary book creates a powerful experience of the Reality and Truth of Ruchira Avatar Adi Da Samraj. Because it so poignantly quotes and clarifies His Teaching and His Life, it has deepened my experience of Him as the Divine Gift established in the cosmic domain.

—GABRIEL COUSENS, M.D.
Author, *Sevenfold Peace* and *Conscious Eating*

Adi Da: The Promised God-Man Is Here *explains the process by which Adi Da Samraj chose to leave the Bright Field in order to fully experience the human condition and re-emerge as the God-Man. In this truly selfless work, He identified our core problem—the "knot of egoity" that separates us from Reality and leads directly to intolerance and non-cooperation between and among individuals, nations, and cultures.*

Adi Da teaches that dissolving the knot is not only a possibility but is the responsibility of every woman and man. He calls upon us to leave our childish and adolescent ways behind, through devotional surrender to God and self-understanding.

—DAN HAMBURG
Former Member of U.S. Congress;
Executive Director, Voice of the Environment

Learn about Avatar Adi Da's Liberating Offering to all: the devotional and Spiritual relationship to Him

The Way of Adidam

Five Steps to an Ecstatic Life of Communion with Real God

A Guide to the Unique Devotional and Spiritual Relationship Offered by the Ruchira Avatar, Adi Da Samraj

A direct and simple summary of each of the fundamental aspects of the Way of Adidam. 194 pp., **$16.95**

I regard the work of Adi Da and his devotees as one of the most penetrating spiritual and social experiments happening on the planet in our era.

—JEFFREY MISHLOVE, Ph.D.
Host, PBS television series, "Thinking Allowed";
Author, *The Roots of Consciousness*

Adi Da's Teachings have tremendous significance for humanity. . . . He represents a foundation and a structure for sanity.

—ROBERT K. HALL, M.D.
Psychiatrist; author, *Out of Nowhere;*
Co-founder, The Lomi School and The Lomi Clinic

We invite you to find out more about

Avatar Adi Da Samraj
and the Way of Adidam

■ Find out about our courses, seminars, events, and retreats by calling the regional center nearest you.

AMERICAS
12040 N. Seigler Rd.
Middletown, CA
95461 USA
1-707-928-4936

PACIFIC-ASIA
12 Seibel Road
Henderson
Auckland 1008
New Zealand
64-9-838-9114

AUSTRALIA
P.O. Box 244
Kew 3101
Victoria
**1800 ADIDAM
(1800-234-326)**

EUROPE-AFRICA
Annendaalderweg 10
6105 AT Maria Hoop
The Netherlands
31 (0)20 468 1442

THE UNITED KINGDOM
P.O. Box 20013
London, England
NW2 1ZA
0208-962-8855

EMAIL: **correspondence@adidam.org**

■ Order books, tapes, and videos by and about Avatar Adi Da Samraj.
1-877-770-0772 (from within North America)
1-707-928-6653 (from outside North America)
order online: **www.adidam.com**

■ Visit us online at: **www.adidam.org**
Explore the online community of Adidam and discover more about Avatar Adi Da and the Way of Adidam.